BATMAN
TANGLES WITH TERROR

written by
MATTHEW K. MANNING

illustrated by
ETHEN BEAVERS

BATMAN created by
BOB KANE with
BILL FINGER

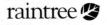
raintree
a Capstone company — publishers for children

Raintree is an imprint of Capstone Global Library
Limited, a company incorporated in England and
Wales having its registered office at 7 Pilgrim
Street, London, EC4V 6LB – Registered company
number: 6695582

www.raintree.co.uk
myorders@raintree.co.uk

STAR38699

Applications for the copyright owner's written
permission should be addressed to the
publisher.

Editor: Anna Butzer
Art Director: Bob Lentz
Graphic Designer: Hilary Wacholz

ISBN 978 1 4747 3751 7
21 20 19 18 17
10 9 8 7 6 5 4 3 2 1

British Library Cataloguing in Publication Data
A full catalogue record for this book is available
from the British Library.

Printed in China.

CONTENTS

REAL NAME: Bruce Wayne

ROLE: Super hero and businessman

BASE: Gotham City

HEIGHT: 1.88m (6' 2")

EYES: Blue

HAIR: Black

ABILITIES: Through years of training, he has obtained peak human strength, speed, reflexes and endurance. He is a skilled scientist, detective and master of disguise.

BACKGROUND: When he was a boy, Bruce Wayne's parents were killed by a mugger. After that, Bruce swore that he would rid Gotham City of the evil that took his parents from him. He began training around the world. After many years he returned to protect Gotham City as Batman.

CHAPTER 1

THE BOY WHO FELL

There once was a little boy who fell down a hole.

It had been a bright day up above. But the hole was dark and deep, and the boy was very much alone. Or at least, he thought he was.

As the boy's eyes adjusted to the darkness, he realized the hole was the entrance to a cave. And there, in the darkest corner of that cave, emerged two tiny eyes. They glowed a colour the boy had never seen before. It was a colour he hoped to never see again.

The boy blinked, and the two eyes became four. The four eyes became eight. He blinked again. Suddenly, the darkness in front of him was filled with beady pinpricks of reflected light.

The boy was terrified.

"Father!" the boy cried out. "Mother! Can anyone hear me?"

That was when the eyes became something else entirely.

That was when the boy first met the bats.

FLAP! FLAP! FLAP!

They swarmed around him. They encircled his body like a tornado. Wind from their leathery wings beat against his cheeks. Their high-pitched screeches pierced his ears!

EEEK! EEEK! EEEK!

He raised his hands to cover his face. It was all he could do to protect himself. The boy closed his eyes and screamed.

AAAAHHHHH!

CHAPTER 2

THE MAN WHO WOKE

Bruce Wayne wakes with a start.

"Sleeping on the job, Master Bruce?"
Alfred Pennyworth says as he walks into
the Batcave. He carries the evening's
freshly prepared dinner.

Bruce doesn't reply to his butler. He simply lets out a quiet breath, as if hoping to exhale his nightmare away. It doesn't seem to work.

"It is past two in the morning," says Alfred. "Consider retiring to the Manor and a proper bed."

Bruce doesn't answer right away. He stands up and walks away from the Batcomputer. Alfred quietly awaits his master's reply. He is used to waiting on Bruce Wayne, in every sense of the word.

"I'm late for my nightly patrol as it is," Bruce says as he slides on his mask. With that, it is as if billionaire Bruce Wayne disappears completely.

Now there is only . . . Batman.

Bruce Wayne may be well known in the social circles of the rich and famous. But as Batman, he is a hero to all of Gotham City. He is a protector, a noble crime fighter who seems almost unreal.

And to the criminals who cross paths with him, he is something more. He is the Dark Knight, the Caped Crusader. In his cape and cowl, he is a thing of shadows come alive.

CHAPTER 3

THE NIGHTMARE THAT LURKED

The Batmobile roars towards Gotham
City, its driver lost in thought. The sleek
car's headlights catch the dark green trees in
passing. The road is lit just enough to allow
Batman to find his way towards his city.

He knows the route. He has taken it hundreds of times before. He drives as if on autopilot, letting the car find the way. All the while, he can't stop thinking about his nightmare.

Why does it continue to haunt me? he wonders. *What does it mean?*

On any other night, Batman would notice the dark figure on the otherwise empty road in front of him. He would see the moon shining down on its fur. He would see its almost impossible size, its giant wings. He would see the hulking shadow that is like a funhouse mirror image of his own silhouette.

But tonight, Batman doesn't see the creature called Man-Bat until it's much too late.

Batman does his best to keep control of the Batmobile. But he's going too fast. He jerks the wheel to the side.

SCREECH!

Batman slams on the brakes. The Batmobile's front tyres stray off the road. Then the back tyres follow suit. Despite his time training with the best drivers money could hire, Batman can't correct the car's course.

CRASH!

The Batmobile smashes through the underbrush of the nearby forest. A tree seems to come out of nowhere. The Dark Knight barely has enough time to press the eject button. Then the sleek car slams into the tree trunk.

CRUNCH!

CHAPTER 4

THE CREATURE HE FACED

Batman's cape billows in the wind as he lands on the soft earth below. He has trained for this. And more than that, he's fought Man-Bat before. The creature was once a scientist named Dr Kirk Langstrom.

Dr Langstrom created a serum to help with his difficulty hearing. But when he tested it, something went wrong. Instead of a cure, it became a disease.

The man became a monster. He changed into a hulking bat creature, more animal than man. Dr Langstrom became a Man-Bat even he could not control.

Batman shakes his head and clenches his jaw.

Where are you hiding? he thinks to himself. *You couldn't have gone far.*

Batman peers into the dark forest surrounding him. He knows that here in the woods, Man-Bat is in his element.

Sure, there are no innocent people
for him to harm. There is no property for
him to destroy. But the thick underbrush
could hide even a creature of his size. The
dark trees and branches would serve as
the perfect cover. Finding Man-Bat, and
bringing him home, will not be easy.

Suddenly, Batman sees eyes glowing
in the forest in front of him. He instantly
recognizes them.

It seems Man-Bat isn't interested in hiding at all. Batman's mind works quickly. He begins debating his next move. He places his hand on his Utility Belt. But he's not thinking about Batarangs or grapnels or gas capsules. Instead, he keeps looking at Man-Bat's eyes.

There is something about those large, glowing eyes. There is something all too familiar about them that makes Batman hesitate. He thinks back to the little boy who fell in the hole.

Thud . . . Thud . . .

Batman's heart pounds as he thinks of those wild bats that swarmed around him all those years ago. He doesn't move. He simply stands still. The Dark Knight seems to freeze in his tracks.

It's then, for the first time in years, that Batman remembers his father's hands. They were the hands he saw lowering the rope down the deep, dark hole. They were the hands that pulled him back out to safety.

Bruce remembers the words he and his father spoke as they hugged.

"Were those monsters, Dad?" He had asked.

"No, Bruce. They were just bats," his father had said. "And because they're bats, they hear everything. The noises you made . . . you just spooked them, that's all."

"But they were so scary," he had replied.

"They were as scared of you, as you were of them," his father had said.

The words echo in Batman's mind – even as Man-Bat makes a break from the tree line.

CHAPTER 5

THE BAT LEFT STANDING

Man-Bat dives at Batman, but the Dark Knight stands his ground. He is no longer that scared little boy who fell. He raises his fists and prepares for impact.

When Man-Bat collides with him, Batman allows himself to roll backwards. In the air, Man-Bat has an advantage. He can get away quickly if need be. Batman knows that his only hope for taking down the beast is to keep him grounded.

RRRAAAHHH!

The hulking creature's jaws snap and snarl. But Batman remains calm. He is no longer afraid of the dark or of bats or of being alone. He has become the very thing that once terrified him so. And it is time to show Man-Bat exactly what that means.

Using the creature's own weight, Batman flips him backwards. For a second, the beast is shocked. It doesn't understand how a simple human can move so quickly. Then Man-Bat slowly picks himself up and shakes the dust out of his fur.

Batman also stands up to face his enemy. His cape drapes around his shoulders. The fight is not man versus animal, as Man-Bat's simple mind had thought. This is a battle between equals. This is a fight between two creatures of the night.

CLICK!

Batman presses a button on a remote control from his Utility Belt. He knows that tonight, he is not the one who needs to be afraid.

HHHHHRRRRRRRNNNNNNNN!!

The sound of the Batmobile's horn blares in Man-Bat's sensitive ears. The car's headlights blind his eyes. He stumbles forward. He moves not like a hulking beast, but like an injured animal.

With a whimper he cowers before Batman. And perhaps for the first time, Man-Bat truly knows fear.

Man-Bat is almost helpless as Batman binds him in a thick cord from his Utility Belt. Batman ties him to a nearby billboard by the side of the road, but there is almost no need to. The creature is defeated, frightened and humbled.

As Batman slips into the cover of the forest, he hears the Gotham City Police arrive.

"How did this creature get here?" one of the officers asks.

"I don't know," the other replies. "But if it could talk, I bet it would be a doozy of a story."

Yes, the Dark Knight thinks with a smile, *a story Man-Bat will likely never tell but will long remember.*

For he knows one thing is certain. When Man-Bat remembers this night – when he recalls this encounter – he will remember that his fear has a name.

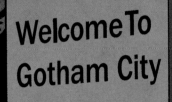

And that name is . . . Batman!

MAN-BAT

REAL NAME: Kirk Langstrom

ROLE: Zoologist

BASE: Gotham City

HEIGHT: 2.24m (7' 4")

EYES: Brown

HAIR: Brown

ABILITIES: After years of taking the serum, Dr Langstrom is able to change into the Man-Bat at any time. He can fly, has sharp claws and can find his way through the air with echolocation. He is also able to create sonic waves that stun people near him.

BACKGROUND: When Kirk was a boy he fell into a deep cavern and was lost for more than six weeks. When the police finally found him, Kirk seemed sad to leave the cave and the creatures that lived there. As an adult, Kirk became a zoologist and an expert on nocturnal mammals. He believed he could lead a medical breakthrough by studying bats. He tested a new serum made from bat glands on himself, and it caused him to turn into a half-human, half-bat creature.

GLOSSARY

billow when something billows it is pushed outward by the wind

clench to hold or squeeze something tightly

collide to crash together forcefully, often at high speed

cower to crouch down in fear

cowl hood

impact striking of one thing against another

serum liquid used to prevent or cure a disease

silhouette outline of something that shows its shape

stumble to trip, or walk in an unsteady way

ABOUT THE AUTHOR

Matthew K. Manning is the author of over 50 books. He has contributed to many comic books as well, including *Teenage Mutant Ninja Turtles: Amazing Adventures*, *Beware the Batman* and the crossover miniseries *Batman/TMNT Adventures*. He currently resides in Asheville, North Carolina, USA, with his wife Dorothy and their two daughters, Lillian and Gwendolyn. Visit him online at www.matthewkmanning.com.

ABOUT THE ILLUSTRATOR

Ethen Beavers is a professional comic book artist from Modesto, California, USA. His best-known works for DC Comics include *Justice League Unlimited* and *Legion of Superheroes in the 31st Century*. He has also illustrated for other top publishers, including Marvel, Dark Horse and Abrams.

WRITING PROMPTS

1. Batman works to protect people and stop villains. Imagine if you were a super hero What would your powers be? What would you do with them? Write about it.

2. Who is a real life super hero to you? Write about this person and explain why you think he or she has super qualities.

3. Batman uses many gadgets from his Utility Belt to capture his foes. Imagine you had your own Utility Belt. List and describe the tools you would carry on it.

DISCUSSION QUESTIONS

1. Bruce was afraid of the bats in the cave, but his father helped him to feel better. What is something you used to be afraid of? How did you overcome your fear?

2. Batman keeps his real identity hidden. If you were a super hero how would you keep your identity a secret?

3. This book uses illustrations to help tell the story. Which illustration do you think helps the reader understand the action the most? Why?

READ THEM ALL